MW01437808

Embracing
the Cycles of
Gratitude
A Personal 30-Day Journey

Vanessa Bolden-Beaver

Copyright © 2023

**Cover and Layout Design
Diverse City**
www.enterthecity.com

All rights reserved. No part of this book may be reproduced or used in any manner without the prior written permission of the copyright owner, except for the use of brief quotations in a book review.

**Gorman House Publishing
Chicago, IL**
www.gormanhousepublishing.com

Preface

As I reflect of childhood memories, I can remember when my mother would yell at me from the kitchen window to come inside because it was time for dinner. My brothers and I would gather around this 6-chair wood table with my parents positioned at the ending seats. Me and my brothers would sit down and begin to talk loudly, laugh, play drums on the table with the utensils, while my mother completed dinner preparations.

My mother would place the food on the table, then my father would say in a deep, authoritative voice, "Okay, okay, that's enough, bow your heads". Everyone would become silent; we would bow our heads preparing for my father to say grace. He would always mention how thankful he was for the food and the hands that prepared it. That prayer of thankfulness has followed me through the years allowing me to expand my vision to see all the many things I am grateful for.

This daily affirmation book was created to help change a person's eyesight from focusing on daily stresses of life such as family issues, business woes, work depression, and daily emotions of rejection and hurt to mention a few.

If we only take the time to "smell the roses" we can see how beautiful every day is no matter the weather or circumstance, we may be in.

If we focus daily on the positive thoughts, the negative ones cannot live and breathe, but they begin to fade away over time.

Everyday we have something to be grateful for.

Something to smile at.

Something to exercise our faith to achieve.

Something to live for.

This 30-day journey was written to help to reset the mind; training it to take bad situations and turn them into positive building blocks of your future.

"Gratitude can transform any situation. It alters your vibrations, moving you from the negative to the positive. It's the quickest, easiest, most powerful way to effect change in your life—this I know for sure."
Oprah Winfrey

"Cultivate the habit of being grateful for every good thing that comes to you, and to give thanks continuously. And because all things have contributed to your advancement, you should include all things in your gratitude."
Ralph Waldo Emerson

Acknowledgements

I want to acknowledge my husband, Jason and my children, Janessa and Jayda, brothers, Richard, Ronald, and Henry Jr., my sisters, Angela and Marcia, and Mother in love, Valeria, my spiritual and inspirational brothers, Marqus and David, and my right hand, Engia, you are my tribe has encouraged, motivated, supported, and believed in me to do what I believed was impossible. Love you all!

I dedicate this book to my parents, Henry and Mary Bolden who has taught me how to be grateful and thankful for all that I have.

Begin your Personal 30 Day Journey

Day 1

I am thankful for all opportunities. My attitude reflects my happiness.

I am thankful for all opportunities that come my way. I let go of the idea that things must be ideal for me to be happy. I recognize that every situation has both challenges and rewards.

Basing my sense of well being on the absence of conflict in my life is futile. There will always be challenges, and I cannot delay my happiness because of their presence.

I believe that success comes to those who take action with what they have at hand. Opportunities for small successes often lead to greater possibilities.

For this reason, I choose to look for the opportunities inherent in every circumstance. Even unpleasant situations can lead to better opportunities that would not have been available without facing the challenge.

I know that challenges teach me the patience and other skills I need in order to make the most of my life. Obstacles help develop my character.

I welcome all challenges and I remain open to the good that awaits me with each new opportunity.

By letting go of the expectation of ease or

perfection, I enable myself to discover the possibilities within every situation. I create my own happiness, even in the midst of challenges.

Self-Reflection Questions:

1. Am I waiting for perfection in order to be happy?
_____
_____
_____
_____

2. Do I view challenges as obstacles or opportunities?
_____
_____
_____
_____

3. What opportunity has come to me unexpectedly because I remained open to finding the good in a tough situation?
_____
_____
_____
_____

Day 2

I am grateful for the abundance that I experience daily.

I am filled with the joy of gratitude for all that I have. I am blessed to have such abundance in my life.

I take time each day to count my many blessings. I am fortunate to enjoy good health, wealth, and happiness. I deserve these things because I act daily to cultivate them. I make my health, finances, and happiness a priority.

My friends and family are another source of abundance. I am the recipient of great love, respect, and admiration. The people in my life are constant reminders of my value to the world. I am innately important and valuable.

Whatever I require, I am provided. All the resources I require to live an exciting and fruitful life are around me. My biggest task is to identify the resources I need and keep my eyes open. Whatever I need is sure to be found quickly and easily. I know what I need and I know how to get it.

While I enjoy unlimited abundance, I avoid the burden of accumulating excessive possessions. I take what I need and remain free of greedy behavior. Living this way keeps my time and conscience free and unburdened.

Today, I give thanks for all that I have. The bounty of the world is mine to enjoy and use as necessary. I am grateful for the abundance that I experience daily.

Self-Reflection Questions:

1. What do I have in my life that fills me with feelings of gratitude?

_____
_____
_____
_____
_____

2. How can I be more open to receiving abundance into my life?

_____
_____
_____
_____
_____

3. How have I impeded receiving abundance?

_____
_____
_____
_____
_____

Day 3

My life overflows with gratitude.

In every situation I face, I have a grateful attitude because I choose to focus on my blessings rather than on my constraints. No matter how dark the clouds get above my head, I embrace thankfulness.

I am grateful because even out of those gray clouds, rain comes, bringing new life into the earth. In the same way, the challenges I face may seem overwhelming, but out of those trials I learn lessons that help me become a better person.

In any situation I face, I rejoice, because there is a reason for everything. I trust that my life is in the hands of my Creator, and as the trials come, so will the solutions. I feel honored when I think that my Creator believes I am strong enough to handle what I am facing.

Humility allows me to be grateful when it would be easy to take things for granted. Sometimes, it may seem that my blessings are simply the result of my hard work or that I am simply entitled to them. In reality, it's only by grace and mercy that I have all of the good things in my life.

I cultivate gratitude within myself because there are people in much worse situations than me. Regardless of what happens, compassion for others always helps me remember my many blessings.

Today, I choose to be glad because a happy outlook can soothe a difficult situation, but an attitude of complaint only makes things more challenging. I give thanks in everything because I am truly blessed.

Self-Reflection Questions:

1. What have I learned from a past trial?
_____
_____
_____
_____
_____
_____

2. What am I thankful for today?
_____
_____
_____
_____
_____
_____

3. In what areas can I be more grateful?
_____
_____
_____
_____
_____
_____

Day 4

I am blessed.

I know that I am blessed. I remind myself to be content with what I have. I cultivate a sense of gratitude and thank others for their kindness.

I share my riches with others. I pitch in when a coworker is swamped and take time to listen when a friend is going through a difficult time. I volunteer in my community and extend my hospitality to newcomers and old friends.

I keep my attention focused on the good things in my life. I avoid fretting about past disappointments or comparing myself to others. I realize that I have all that I need to be happy in this present moment.

I acknowledge my potential and accomplishments. Thinking about my victories builds my confidence and inspires me to aim higher.

I treasure my health and wellbeing. With a strong body and sound mind, I can take on challenges and fulfill my dreams.

I value my family and friends. I let them know that they are a vital part of my life.

I appreciate my education, and the opportunity to do meaningful work. My knowledge, wisdom, and skills help me to contribute to society and provide for my family.

I enjoy the beauty that surrounds me. I take a walk around my neighborhood to marvel at nature and renew my energy. I listen to music that eases my tension and cheers me up.

Today, I count my blessings. I treat each day as a precious gift.

Self-Reflection Questions:

1. How can I spot blessings that initially look like hardships?

_____
_____
_____
_____

2. What is one blessing that I tend to take for granted?

_____
_____
_____
_____

3. How does counting my blessings attract more happiness and good fortune?

_____
_____
_____
_____

Day 5

I give thanks for 10 things each day.

There is so much that I am thankful for. As I lie in bed each morning, my mind instantly starts to run through all that I can say 'thanks' about.

I know that I could spend all day listing the many things that spark my gratitude, but instead I focus on 10 things each day.

When I open my eyes and see the sun peeping through the cracks in the window, I give thanks for a new day. As I wiggle my toes and stretch my fingers, I am grateful for having them to help me do good things for others.

I find meaning in the simple occurrences of each day. As I wait on the traffic light to turn green, I am thankful for the opportunity to say a kind word or give a kind gesture to another road user.

Although I can easily find 10 different things to be grateful for each day, I always include thanks for loved ones and the opportunity to live right with others. I recognize that people around me who show me love help to make life worth living. I also recognize that having the opportunity to show love to others is something I am meant to do.

Today, I commit to remaining eternally grateful. I commit to being truly thankful for all the blessings that come my way, even if I fail to see it right away. I know there is much to be thankful for!

Self-Reflection Questions:

1. Do I ever neglect to say thanks for blessings?

_____
_____
_____
_____
_____

2. Can my blessings be blessings to others?

_____
_____
_____
_____
_____

3. Do I encourage those around me to express thanks to the Creator every day?

_____
_____
_____
_____
_____

Day 6

I treasure life's little moments.

I feel joyful and content. I appreciate small pleasures and everyday miracles. Luxury goods and exotic destinations sound nice, but I have what I need close to home.

I decide what is worth cherishing. I listen to my heart instead of chasing after status symbols or comparing myself to others.

I delight in the company of my loved ones. I take my friends out to dinner and plan outings with my family. I hug my children and hold hands with my spouse.

I nourish my body and mind with delicious whole foods. I savor a bowl of hot vegetable soup with a slice of crusty sourdough bread. I snack on toasted almonds and kale chips. I quench my thirst with pure water or green tea.

I relax in a warm bath or soft hammock. I remove my shoes and spread my toes out wide. I play gentle instrumental music while I am cooking or commuting.

I take time to laugh and play. I remember that it is okay to be silly sometimes.

I am enchanted by the sights and sounds of nature. I watch squirrels play and listen to birds sing. I work in my garden or take a walk through the local park. I bask in the warmth of the morning sun.

I know that simple things can be magnificent.

Today, I am attuned to the ordinary pleasures and experiences that surround me. Each happy and rewarding moment adds up to a satisfying life.

Self-Reflection Questions:

1. What are three things that are more important than money?

_____
_____
_____
_____
_____

2. How does slowing down help me to appreciate each day more?

_____
_____
_____
_____
_____

3. What is one beautiful thing I tend to overlook?

_____
_____
_____
_____
_____

Day 7

Blessings surround me every day.

Every moment of every day, I see endless blessings around me. I consider everything associated with life to be something special.

When I look into the eyes of my laughing children, I feel blessed to share that joy. I know that many others may not be able to experience that. I treasure every opportunity to spend time with my kids.

I take the time to learn from each experience and feel fortunate to be able to learn life lessons along the way.

Taking in the fresh air at sunrise brings me so much happiness. I feel my lungs expand. That reminds me that I am blessed to be alive. I am blessed to have good health and the chance to feel nature.

I take pleasure in tending to my garden. My family enjoys many meals from that garden. Knowing that I can provide for them makes me feel blessed and honored.

All my senses are alive. My eyes, ears, and nose are able to enjoy all the world has to offer. I am truly grateful to be in this position. I am conscious that everything I am able to do is because I am truly blessed.

Today, I avoid taking things for granted. Even the simple things are truly appreciated because I know others may not have access to them. I avoid complaining about the have-nots and celebrate everything I have. Each day, I look forward to the chance to give thanks!

Self-Reflection Questions:

1. Do I encourage my friends and family to give thanks for all the blessings in their lives?

_____
_____
_____
_____
_____
_____

2. Do I make it a point to share my blessings with loved ones?

_____
_____
_____
_____
_____
_____

3. Am I able to be a blessing to others, especially those in need?

_____
_____
_____
_____
_____
_____

Day 8

I feel truly appreciated when others thank me.

I give a lot of worth to the word 'thanks.' I love to hear it from others because it means I am living up to my Creator's expectations of me. I know I am in the world to make a positive impact on others, and I appreciate when others recognize it.

As people go through the motions of life, saying 'thanks' is a gesture that is often taken for granted - without much thought being given to it. But I am still happy to hear it because I know deep down it is being expressed by someone that I positively impact.

I appreciate the gratitude of others.

The appreciation I feel when I do something positive for someone is just as good as the act itself. When someone tells me how thankful they are, I feel inspired to do another good act.

I am propelled to make other people happy when I recognize the positive effect my actions have on someone.

When my kids say 'thanks' for a gift or a late-night snack, I know it is something they truly appreciate. It warms their hearts and shows them that I really love them.

Today, I embrace the positive feeling of being appreciated. Even when others forget to express their appreciation for my positive gestures, I know that the impact of the gesture is still just as great. I endeavor to continue doing positive things for others.

Self-Reflection Questions:

1. Do I say 'thanks' to others often enough?
_____
_____
_____
_____
_____
_____

2. Can I feel the gratitude of others even if they don't thank me?
_____
_____
_____
_____
_____
_____

3. Am I treated differently by others when I continue to show my appreciation and gratitude?
_____
_____
_____
_____
_____
_____

Day 9

I can always find something to feel thankful for.

Today is bountiful and full of blessings. The smiles on my children's faces, my partner's demonstrations of love, and the feelings my home provokes make me feel like I am the luckiest person on the planet. My eyes, ears, and heart are wide open to the riches that surround me.

Each day, the sky presents me with a unique display of light, dark, and color, from sunrise to sunset. When I am outdoors, I see the beautiful plants, trees, and flowers. Their essence surrounds me. I have so many things to be thankful for.

My physical health sustains me throughout the day. My eyes allow me to complete my work. When I hear the sounds of my co-workers typing on their computer keyboards, I am reminded of my own personal work ethic.

I am thankful for my body, which ensures I can move freely and travel from place to place. I keep my arms and legs strong by walking, biking, and swimming. I am thankful for my strength.

Today, I am thankful for an abundance of blessings. I am grateful for my wonderful life.

Self-Reflection Questions:

1. What am I most thankful for?

_____
_____
_____
_____
_____

2. How often do I allow myself to take notice of the wonderful people, places, and things that I have in my life?

_____
_____
_____
_____
_____

3. What can I do to show thanks for all that I have?

_____
_____
_____
_____
_____

Day 10

I am full of gratitude.

I have so much to be thankful for. All of my needs and many of my wants are met. People who care about me surround me and I am aware of their loving presence. Because of this, I am full of gratitude.

So many people in this world go without basic needs: food, shelter, or clean water. Many struggle just to get by each day. When I think about these things, I remember how blessed I am. Regardless of what my future may hold, today I have food, shelter, and clean water and those gifts are worthy of my gratitude.

Each day, I take a few moments to remind myself of my many blessings. I think of the people who love me. I take a moment to mentally send love and gratitude to all of them in return.

I remember all of the ways in which life is easy for me. I have gifts and talents to share. Many things come easily to me, even when I feel challenged by my life. Other things come less easily to me, but I know that each one is an opportunity to learn.

I intentionally cultivate thankfulness for life's challenging situations too.

If I ever feel like I have little to be grateful for, and counting my blessings seems not to help, I go out of my way to do a good turn for someone else. By being helpful to others, I remind myself that the world is an abundant place. And when I remember this, I am grateful.

Today, I am thankful for the blessings in my life. I take time to be conscious of each of them. With all of this abundance surrounding me, I am full of gratitude.

Self-Reflection Questions:

1. What can I be thankful for today?
_____
_____
_____
_____
_____

2. How can I be of service to someone today?
_____
_____
_____
_____
_____

3. In what ways does being helpful to others increase my own gratitude?
_____
_____
_____
_____
_____

Day 11

I take small steps in life and appreciate the time I have.

Life is not a race. I can take the time to appreciate everything around me and be fully present in each moment.

I rejoice each day, whether sunny or cloudy, because this day is mine and I enjoy just being present.

The morning breeze and the smell of brewing coffee sing sweet songs to my senses. I fully enjoy the fresh feeling I have as I take my morning shower; the water washing over my body feels satisfying. I am in no rush.

I prepare for the day and take the time to enjoy the process even if it is the same routine as many times before. Today is different in subtle ways. Each day as I settle in for the evening, I reflect on my day with a happy mindset.

I am fully present in my day, and I choose not to rush through any part of it. I recognize the slight differences in this day and appreciate each moment.

I take the time to reflect daily, and I enjoy re-living the beauty of the day. Each day is a joy, so I celebrate the good times and appreciate life's lessons as they unravel.

Self-Reflection Questions:

1. Have I been fully present in my day?
_____
_____
_____
_____
_____

2. Have I taken the time to notice the subtle differences in the day?
_____
_____
_____
_____
_____

3. Have I taken the time to reflect on my day?
_____
_____
_____
_____
_____

Day 12

Winning reminds me that I am blessed.

I relish in victory whenever I am fortunate to have it. Although it is natural to celebrate winning, I take time out to be thankful. Each success that I experience reminds me that I am blessed.

My ability to be successful at business ventures means I have the skills to do it. Each morning, I give thanks for my natural talents and skills.

I sharpen the skills that keep me in winning mode. The more time I spend refining my abilities the greater the likelihood of ongoing success in my life.

I avoid overlooking the support I get from loved ones in my quest for personal accomplishment. Their emotional support and encouragement help to quell my fears. Family members are a blessing because they give me confidence to persevere.

It is a blessing to be able to push through challenges with resolve. Whenever I feel my tenacity waning, I take a moment to refocus on the goal at hand and get back on track

Today, I am grateful for each blessing that comes my way. The pride that I feel when I achieve greatness is quickly replaced with gratitude for the opportunity.

Self-Reflection Questions:

1. How do I respond when I am unable to attain something that I work hard for?

_____
_____
_____
_____
_____
_____

2. What are some of the blessings that I am most thankful for?

_____
_____
_____
_____
_____
_____

3. How often do I say thanks to others for their help?

_____
_____
_____
_____
_____
_____

Day 13

I practice gratitude daily.

I know that in order to have a happy life, gratitude is necessary and thankfulness requires cultivation. Therefore, I practice gratitude daily.

I take time before bed to remind myself of all the things for which I am thankful. Reflecting on my day, I consider my positive actions and the kindness of others throughout the day. In a very literal way, I count my many blessings.

Also, I notice the gifts that come to me through no action of my own. Perhaps I have a special skill or talent, or maybe I was born into a loving family. Whatever the blessing, I take note and say a small prayer of thanks.

To further cultivate my gratitude, I may also choose to engage in spiritual pursuits. Whether I practice at home or at a formal place of worship, with ritual or with spontaneity, I ensure that my spiritual life includes many thanks. I take every opportunity to experience my gratitude.

I know that many people go through life feeling unloved or unwelcome. And with the challenges inherent in living, I can easily see how these feelings could arise. However, I know that even in my darkest of times, I have much to be thankful for. And on my best days, my heart overflows naturally.

Today, I make an effort to remember my many blessings. My life is always better when I live with a thankful heart. Therefore, I practice gratitude daily.

Self-Reflection Questions:

1. What are some of the blessings in my life right now?

_____
_____
_____
_____
_____
_____

2. What can I be thankful for about my family?

_____
_____
_____
_____
_____
_____

3. Do I have any skills or talents for which I can be grateful? If so, what are they?

_____
_____
_____
_____
_____
_____

Day 14

Blessings follow me wherever I go.

In all things, I am blessed and I make it a point to take notice of all the good in my life. Even if I experience challenging events, I always remember how blessed I am.

I always have plenty of whatever I need. And often, I have more than enough. I am loved abundantly and I have plentiful love to give in return.

Infinite resources are at my fingertips. In the realm of money, I always have enough to cover my basic needs and to meet many of my desires, too.

If I experience times when I feel a lack of abundance, I remind myself that, in truth, I have all that I require. Whether I am employed or unemployed, partnered or single, with lots of kids or no kids at all, I feel blessed in a multitude of ways.

Nothing I can do can destroy or wash away the many blessings that come my way. And to be fully satisfied with life, all I have to do is remember the abundance that is available to me.

My universe is plentiful and my heart is abundant. Blessings come to me freely, and I cultivate gratitude for it.

Today, I make time to contemplate the ways in which I am a blessed. I regularly experience gratitude for all of the wonderful things in my life. And I seek out opportunities to demonstrate this gratitude by living with a sense of abundance.

Self-Reflection Questions:

1. How have blessings manifested in my life in the past few weeks?

_____
_____
_____
_____
_____

2. What are three things I can be thankful for today?

_____
_____
_____
_____
_____

3. What are some positive surprises that have arisen from events I initially perceived as negative?

_____
_____
_____
_____
_____

Day 15

The more grateful I am, the more reasons I find to be grateful.

Being grateful comes so easily to me. I find reasons to be grateful every day.

When I first wake up, I mentally list the things I am grateful for in my life. Anytime I experience a challenge, I remind myself of my many blessings. Being grateful makes my life richer and easier.

Being thankful for the little things in life is a remarkable way to live. I appreciate the little things. I find that the more grateful I am, the more reasons I find to be grateful.

Being grateful is not always easy, but if I find a situation challenging, I purposely look for something positive in it. Invariably, I can find something good. Now I can smile at any situation and realize it is a gift.

When I lie down at night, I again reflect on things I am thankful for. This simple habit always makes me happy and fills me with hope. My life is so wonderful.

I am so blessed. My blessings are too numerous to even count. I am the happiest person in the world. I am continuously receiving good things in life. I appreciate all that I have and wish everyone could be as fortunate as I am.

Today, I view my life with gratitude. I find the positive in each situation. I see the excellence in every person. And I feel that the world is good. The more grateful I am, the more reasons I find to be grateful.

Self-Reflection Questions:

1. What am I grateful for in my life? What else could I be grateful for?

_____
_____
_____
_____
_____
_____

2. How would I benefit from a stronger sense of gratitude?

_____
_____
_____
_____
_____
_____

3. How can I cultivate more gratitude?

_____
_____
_____
_____
_____
_____

Day 16

I start my day with gratitude.

I begin each day with a feeling of love and thankfulness in my heart. I avoid the negative thoughts that bring my day down to a harmful level.

I see each new day as a chance to say thank you to the universe.

I count the blessings that surround me and fill my life. I appreciate the people who make my life easier and better.

I am thankful for my friends and family every morning.

I am grateful for my work, home, neighborhood and relationships. I see how others suffer around me, and I focus on peace.

Gratitude fills my spirit, and my joy increases.

I appreciate the five senses that help me experience this planet. I am happy I can connect with nature, people, and animals.

My morning is complete because gratitude occupies my thoughts.

I use my morning to appreciate my life and accomplishments. I reflect on my experiences and past. I make plans for the future to help my job and family. I focus on ideas that uplift all of us and help us reach new goals.

Today, I begin my morning with gratitude and peace in

my mind. I see how my attitude affects my entire day, so my morning is a time of reflection.

Self-Reflection Questions:

1. How can I find time during a busy morning to show gratitude?

_____
_____
_____
_____
_____

2. How can I teach my family to stop and say thank you each day?

_____
_____
_____
_____
_____

3. What can I do to banish the negative thoughts and experiences that can affect my mornings?

_____
_____
_____
_____
_____

Day 17

My humble beginnings remind me to practice gratitude.

Experiences in my life help to shape my attitude of gratitude. Having humble beginnings reminds me that achievements are blessings instead of entitlements.

Being humble amidst success is a lesson taught from my childhood. My approach is to be gracious in victory instead of boastful. It helps to keep me grounded so I avoid appearing conceited and self-righteous.

Knowing what it feels like to be in need reminds me to be thankful. I use my past situations to fuel my desire to help others.

I am grateful for the opportunity to assist others. I am able to cater to their needs because I understand their experiences firsthand. Those situations remind me of where I am coming from and the effort it takes to stay where I am.

Growing up having less than enough helps me to appreciate sharing now. I place a lot of value on being able to share with special people in my life.

Whenever I am able to, I invite friends and family to share a meal with me. I use those times to express to them how important they are to me. I give thanks for them by embracing them with loving kindness.

Today, I commit to practicing gratitude regardless of my circumstances. My life is filled with opportunities to be thankful. My rewards are richer when I take the time to be sincerely grateful.

Self-Reflection Questions:

1. In what ways can I show gratitude to people who help me along the way?

_____
_____
_____
_____
_____
_____

2. How do I make adjustments when I find myself being ungrateful?

_____
_____
_____
_____
_____
_____

3. What value do I get from sharing my past experiences with my kids?

_____
_____
_____
_____
_____
_____

Day 18

Thankfulness helps me to take success in stride.

Each time I achieve success, I take a moment to acknowledge the feeling it gives me. I focus on the value that the achievement adds to my life. When I allow myself to be present in the moment, I am able to give thanks for the things that I attain.

Thankfulness helps me to remain humble amidst the greatest victories. I remind myself that each thing I am able to do is a result of a blessing.

I avoid taking any of the good things in life for granted. When I take the time to experience gratitude, I am able to honor the true value of the goodness that I receive. Each time I achieve a goal feels like the first time because I remain thankful.

Gratitude encourages me to avoid having an inflated ego with each success. I recognize that each goal I go after requires that I repeat the process of centering myself.

Taking myself back to that feeling of hunger reminds me that there are few promises in life. Hard work and humility make dreams a reality over and over.

Today, I am thankful for the blessings of life. I am committed to maintaining humbleness so each success feels like the first one. My achievements are sweeter because I take the time to acknowledge their positive impact on my life.

Self-Reflection Questions:

1. How can I remind myself to maintain humility?

_____
_____
_____
_____
_____
_____

2. How do I ensure ongoing gratitude when I am unable to achieve a target?

_____
_____
_____
_____
_____
_____

3. What external sources serve as positive influences for me?

_____
_____
_____
_____
_____
_____

Day 19

I accept compliments with grace and gratitude.

I am thankful each time someone lets me know of their appreciation. These situations help remind me what I have to offer the world, whether it's kindness, aesthetic appeal, or practical skills. Therefore, I accept compliments with grace and gratitude.

I look at each compliment as a gift. When someone goes out of their way to be kind to me, I want to accept their gift graciously. When someone gives me a physical gift, I am always sure to say, "Thank you," so why not feel pleased and say it when they give me the gift of praise?

When I accept compliments with grace and gratitude, I also find myself complimenting others more easily and frequently. This spreads happiness.

Like a stone dropped into a pond, when I accept a compliment, positive feelings and actions radiate out from me and touch the lives of other people.

Although I may sometimes feel tempted to brush off praise, I remember that most people are offering it authentically. They truly believe that I deserve their praise. So instead of deflecting their affirmations, I am sure to say, "Thank you."

Today, I am gracious when receiving compliments. I am thankful each time someone chooses to give me a compliment. Each day, I practice saying, "Thank you" to praise, instead of deflecting it.

Self-Reflection Questions:

1. How do I feel when I receive a compliment?
_____
_____
_____
_____
_____

2. Can I choose to say "Thank you," regardless of how I feel about the praise?
_____
_____
_____
_____
_____

3. How can I show grace and gratitude when someone compliments me?
_____
_____
_____
_____
_____

Day 20

In my alone time, I consider things I am grateful for.

Every day is a day of thanksgiving. In the hustle and bustle of life, it is easy to overlook blessings. But I set aside time each day to consider the things I am grateful for.

At times, I invite my kids to share my alone time. I ask them to list things they are thankful for. This bonding activity brings us closer together. It also teaches them to avoid taking things for granted.

Even on difficult days, I give thanks that it is not any worse. I acknowledge that so many others have it worse than me. That mindset helps me to build the drive and will to keep going.

I take the time to express thanks for my tough situations. They teach me perseverance, forgiveness, and creativity. I feel my character building with each challenge I face.

My resolve grows each day after I list the things I am thankful for. I feel more and more invincible.

I see every situation as a blessing. There are some that are tougher than others. But I appreciate every learning experience I get. I admire the person I am becoming.

Today, I find blessings in both my good days and bad days. I commit to finding something positive in every situation. I am grateful regardless of the circumstances I face.

Self-Reflection Questions:

1. Are there difficulties that are too hard for me to overlook?

_____
_____
_____
_____
_____
_____

2. Do I feel refreshed and reenergized after every thanksgiving session I hold?

_____
_____
_____
_____
_____
_____

3. How do I handle situations where others display ungratefulness?

_____
_____
_____
_____
_____
_____

Day 21

I see the best in others and appreciate them for it.

Because I am interested in developing strong relationships with people, I let go of the idea that individuals must be perfect to be accepted. I have flaws and want people to love me regardless. I extend that same respect to others.

In seeking the best in people, I strive to remember that there are no bad traits. Issues that challenge relationships are merely the flip side of more positive qualities.

If my co-worker is stubborn, for instance, he is probably also determined and consistent. If my daughter is emotional, she is likely also sensitive and creative. I choose to focus on the positive aspects of the people I love.

I also strive to empower others to become their very best. I point out their good qualities both to them and to others, knowing that people will live up to whatever they believe to be true.

I let go of the desire to berate people for their shortcomings and, instead, try to build up the good that is already there.

I remember that everyone, including me, is a work in progress. When a sculptor creates a work of art, he often throws the same batch of clay many times before the piece begins to take the shape he envisions beneath his hands.

Likewise, people require time and the patient touch of

the Creator to reach their full potential. I let go and just enjoy the process of watching them develop, fully believing in the beauty of the final product.

Self-Reflection Questions:

1. Do I understand that my loved ones are also works in progress?

_____
_____
_____
_____

2. Do I focus on the positive side of my loved ones' character traits?

_____
_____
_____
_____

3. How can I empower those I love?

_____
_____
_____
_____

Day 22

Some of my greatest blessings are invisible.

Houses and cars are useful, but some of my greatest blessings are invisible. I devote time each day to spotting inward and outward blessings.

My health is precious. Being fit and strong enables me to provide for my family and hike through the woods. I make choices that help me to lead a long and active life. That means plenty of rest, exercise, and green vegetables.

My peace of mind is also priceless. I crave the happiness and satisfaction that comes with knowing I am loved.

The quality of my life also has a spiritual dimension. I engage in practices that are meaningful for me. I surround myself with people who provide me with guidance and encouragement.

My eyes make me aware of many delightful things, but I also count on my ears, nose, and fingers. I pay attention to beautiful sounds, scents, and textures. I listen for bird songs and church bells. I stop to smell flowers and newly cut grass. I dip my hand in cool water.

I focus on my breath to turn my attention inward. I sit down to meditate or pause during my daily activities. I examine the causes of my good feelings and give thanks for them.

To connect with the world around me, I slow down. I close my eyes and let my child's laughter or a favorite symphony fill my mind.

Today, I celebrate the blessings I cannot see. My heart overflows with gratitude and joy.

Self-Reflection Questions:

1. How do I keep material goods in perspective?

___
___
___
___
___

2. What are some intangible items that make my life better?

___
___
___
___
___

3. How can I become more grateful for all my blessings?

___
___
___
___
___

Day 23

I can always find something to be thankful for.

I welcome the small gifts that life gives me each day. I acknowledge the beauty that is around me in nature and in people.

I am fortunate to live in a place that has the ability to grow beautiful flowers. I appreciate the perfume that I smell from those blooming flowers.

I am appreciative of the kindness that I receive when I encounter a stranger. I realize that I am lucky because I have the privilege to meet another person who is kind without reason.

I strive to keep an open and positive state of mind. With an open mind I can clearly see the blessings in my daily life. A positive mind can turn most disappointments into life lessons that are beneficial for my future.

Someone is always going to be better off than me, but there is always going to be someone worse off than me too.

I am thankful for what I have because I know there is someone out there who has much less than me. I know there are others fighting to just survive.

Today, I recognize that being grateful for the life I have rewards my soul with contentment and happiness. I am thankful for all the wonderful people and things in my life.

Self-Reflection Questions:

1. What am I most thankful for today?

_____
_____
_____
_____
_____
_____

2. What are the small gifts I have encountered today?

_____
_____
_____
_____
_____
_____

3. How can I show my appreciation for my blessings?

_____
_____
_____
_____
_____
_____

Day 24

Each day I am grateful for simple things.

Every day that I am here on earth, I am filled with wonder about everything around me. Intense gratitude rises in me at the sound of a child's voice, the fragrance of flowers in the air and the sight of dew-laden grass in the morning.

In a world stuffed with material goods, sometimes I feel challenged to just feel grateful in my own space with my own possessions and the simple things in life. But I remind myself to look around and find what brings me feelings of joy and thankfulness.

When the tough days come along, I think of the smile on my friend's face or I notice the sound of the birds singing in the early evening. My thoughts lead me back to feeling gratitude for these pure sources of light in my life.

The simplest things have the greatest value to me. The comfortable, old stuffed chair in the living room and a glass of fresh orange juice in the morning remind me that I have so much to be thankful for. Each day the sun rises and I am here to see it, I feel grateful.

Life gets pretty complicated sometimes. When it does, I re-focus myself and acknowledge the contentment I find in simplicity. After a hard day's work, I indulge in a glass of iced tea and put my feet up. And I am grateful for these small moments.

Today, I acknowledge all the wondrous yet simple things that surround me. I notice my children's bright eyes, my spouse's facial expressions, and the beauty of nature. I am so grateful every day for simple things in my life.

Self-Reflection Questions:

1. Each day, do I take note of something I am grateful for?

_____
_____
_____
_____
_____
_____

2. How can I ensure that I am spending a few minutes every day reflecting on the blessings in my life?

_____
_____
_____
_____
_____
_____

3. At this very moment, what am I grateful for?

_____
_____
_____
_____
_____
_____

Day 25

My life is full of blessings.

My world is filled with good things. I choose to focus on the positive and ponder the great things that I have in my life.

I awake each day with a fresh vision of how blessed I am this day.

I am thankful for the current weather, regardless of sun, clouds or rain. I appreciate the warmth that comes from the sun and the beautiful flowers that arise from the rain.

I have positive relationships. I am a good friend, spouse, and sibling. I do my part to ensure my relationships are healthy and uplifting. I have great love for my friends and family.

I am thankful for my occupation and the chance to earn a living. The income I earn keeps food on the table and a roof over my head. I look at the bright side in everything that I do at work, even if it is sometimes boring.

Today, I make a conscious effort to take a look at everything in my life just a little bit closer. In this way, I can see more clearly the blessings of those things I often take for granted.

As I do this today and each day, I gain a new appreciation and insight into the wonders of life.

Self-Reflection Questions:

1. What are some areas of my life in which I have difficulty seeing the bright side?

_____
_____
_____
_____
_____
_____

2. How can I show my appreciation for the blessings that come my way?

_____
_____
_____
_____
_____
_____

3. Are there any ways in which I can pass on blessings to others? How?

_____
_____
_____
_____
_____
_____

Day 26

I am thankful that I get to live another day.

Each day is unique and a blessing to experience. Even those days that seem negative have valuable lessons to teach. I take each day in stride. There are many subtle reasons to be thankful for each and every day.

Each day is another opportunity to share time and experiences with those I love. The closeness of my friends and family keeps me going during challenging times and makes me smile during good times. Each day I am able to spend with those I love is a worthwhile day.

Living for another day means I can enjoy the beauty of nature. It is ever-changing and a constant source of amazement to me. I feel at peace when I experience the natural world.

Each morning I wake up with anticipation of what lies ahead. It is impossible to predict what life may bring, which makes my life so interesting.

Another day on Earth is another day to rejoice!

I understand that life is short and passes quickly. I am determined to make the most of each day. I am free from worry and concern. The prospect of living another day fills me with excitement.

Today, I look forward to another interesting and meaningful day. I use my time wisely and enjoy the process of living. I face challenges directly and with a smile. I am thankful that I get to live another day.

Self-Reflection Questions:

1. What have a learned from the challenging times in my life.

_____
_____
_____
_____
_____
_____

2. When have I felt hopeless in the past? Why do things eventually improve?

_____
_____
_____
_____
_____
_____

3. What do I have to look forward to in my life?

_____
_____
_____
_____
_____
_____

Day 27

My blessings are innumerable.

I receive countless blessings each day. When I stop to consider my highpoints in life, I am in awe by them. My list of successes far exceeds any negative occurrences in my life.

Having basic abilities is a blessing that many take for granted. My healthy body and mind allow me to accomplish important things each day. I make the most of my time and am thankful when I am able to achieve daily tasks and goals.

My hard work results in recognition from my employer. Although my efforts are what lead to success, I still recognize the acknowledgement as a blessing .

Whenever I feel the urge to complain or express disappointment, I remind myself that I am blessed. Even when I am in the midst of a trial, I pause and think about all the benefits of life that I enjoy.

I find blessings in the most unexpected places. When I stare into the eyes of a hungry child, I am thankful for the chance to offer a meal.

That chance to help someone is a blessing in itself. It is an exercise in humility that helps me to be appreciative. I enjoy learning helpful life lessons.

Today, I am thrilled about all the blessings I experience each day. I am a firm believer in finding the good in each situation. I continue to give thanks for all the positive things that life throws my way.

Self-Reflection Questions:

1. How do I correct my behavior when I find myself complaining?

_____
_____
_____
_____
_____
_____

2. What inspires positive change in my life?

_____
_____
_____
_____
_____
_____

3. How do I turn a negative situation into a positive one?

_____
_____
_____
_____
_____
_____

Day 28

I take time to reflect on my blessings.

I am a blessed person because I have more than I could ever imagine. The things I love and enjoy the most are things I would never have been able to provide for myself. Therefore, I am blessed.

Acknowledging that I am blessed is the most important element of living a life of gratitude. Daily, I take time to sit down and think about the things I love the most in the world. My family, my children, and even my material possessions are all blessings.

There is nothing I can do to earn or deserve my blessings. Likewise, there is nothing I can do to make myself unworthy of them.

The beauty of blessings is that they are gifts given to me by my Creator simply out of love. Blessings are the way in which I am shown how much I am loved and how big my purpose really is.

I am blessed even when my bank account is low or things do not seem to go my way. Just having air to breathe is a gift. When I consider all that I have been given as a blessing, I overflow with gratitude.

I make it a point to stop each day and look around me. Wherever I am, whether at home or away, there is so much beauty around me, even in the mundane things.

Today, I choose to take a step back and cultivate an awareness of my blessings. I slow down enough to grasp the fragility of life and the gift that it is to have one. When I take time to count my blessings, I experience true gratitude.

Self-Reflection Questions:

1. What am I thankful for today?

_____
_____
_____
_____
_____
_____

2. How can I keep from taking my many gifts for granted?

_____
_____
_____
_____
_____
_____

3. What does it mean to be blessed?

_____
_____
_____
_____
_____

Day 29

Sunsets remind me to be thankful for life.

The end of each day signals the close of a chapter. As I reflect while watching the sun set, I am reminded to be grateful for my daily blessings.

Making it successfully through a rough day means that I have strengths. I acknowledge my abilities as things to be thankful for.

Having a difficult job means having a chance to persevere and overcome. Looking back at the professional road blocks and my ability to pass them fills me with pride. As the sun sets on my victories, I commit to pushing even harder tomorrow.

The closing of one day signals the potential for a new one. I believe that being thankful at the end of each day prepares me for whatever comes my way later on.

When I look at the setting sun, I see a promise for a new day that is even brighter than the current one. I await what life has in store for me in happy anticipation. Experiencing the rotation of the sun reminds me to live my life to the fullest.

Today, the sun sets on my accomplishments of the day and prepares me for even greater opportunities in the future. I commit to making the most of my days and expressing gratitude for even the smallest blessings.

Self-Reflection Questions:

1. In what other situations do I find myself expressing gratitude for life?

_____
_____
_____
_____
_____

2. In what other ways do I interact with nature to find personal inspiration?

_____
_____
_____
_____
_____

3. What are some things that I always take the time to give thanks for?

_____
_____
_____
_____
_____

Day 30

I am blessed to exist in a beautiful world.

I love the world I live in!

Everything that surrounds me allows me to think of how beautiful this creation called Nature and the human race actually are. I believe that there is a spark of positive energy in even the most negative situation.

I recognize that there is much darkness in the world - war, hate and anger are real. But I also know that behind every bit of darkness is a shimmer of light waiting for the right moment to break through.

The world often seems darkest right before the dawn. Sure enough, though, dawn comes again after even the darkest hour.

When I wake up each morning, I feel blessed because I know something great awaits me. I take every opportunity given to me to show others how beautiful life can be. When I am successful at stirring up positive energy, that great feeling I get is incomparable.

I feel blessed when I have the opportunity to make a child smile. The world feels like a more beautiful place when a sad child starts to smile again. I am uplifted when I bring joy and laughter to my family. The love in their eyes shines even brighter as I bring more beauty to their world.

Today, I see the beauty all around me. I extract something good from every situation because I know it is always there. I know that beneath it all, the world is a wonderful place!

Self-Reflection Questions:

1. Am I accepting when I lose someone or something dear to me?

_____
_____
_____
_____
_____
_____

2. Can I embrace the beauty of the world when I am attacked with negativity?

_____
_____
_____
_____
_____
_____

3. Do I teach others the importance of making the most of every moment?

_____
_____
_____
_____
_____
_____

Notes

Notes

Notes

Notes